SCHOLASTIC

Teaching With Favorite Tomie dePaola Books

BY LAURIE DEANGELIS
AND REBECCA DEANGELIS CALLAN

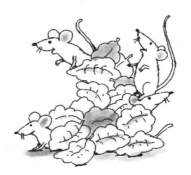

NEW YORK • TORONTO • LONDON • AUCKLAND • SYDNEY
MEXICO CITY • NEW DELHI • HONG KONG • BUENOS AIRES

Teaching
Resources

Chris & Julie—aboosta!
Mom and Dad—all that nudging finally paid off. Thanks.

L P D

To my family—who taught me what's important
Nana and Pap—who taught me where to look
Scott—who teaches me still

R A D C

A special thanks to…

Tomie dePaola—for creating books that make the heart sing
Pam Fagan—for contributing an idea for teaching with
The Cloud Book

Cover reprinted with permission of Simon & Schuster Books for Young Readers, an imprint of Simon & Schuster Children's Publishing Division from STREGA NONA by Tomie dePaola. Copyright © 1975 by Tomie dePaola.

Cover from THE LEGEND OF THE INDIAN PAINTBRUSH by Tomie dePaola, copyright © 1988 by Tomie dePaola. Used by permission of G.P. Putnam's Sons, a division of Penguin Young Readers Group, a Member of Penguin Group (USA) Inc., 345 Hudson St., NY, NY 10014. All rights reserved.

Cover from THE ART LESSON by Tomie dePaola, copyright © 1989 by Tomie dePaola. Used by permission of G.P. Putnam's Sons, a division of Penguin Young Readers Group, a Member of Penguin Group, (USA) Inc., 345 Hudson Street, NY, NY 10014. All rights reserved.

"Meet Tomie dePaola," adapted from *The Big Book of Picture-Book Authors and Illustrators* by James Preller. Copyright © 2001 by James Preller. Photo of Tomie dePaola courtesy of Penguin Putnam, Suki Coughlin.

"Loving" from TOGETHER WE ARE TOGETHER by St. Brigid's Head Start Children. Copyright © 1992 by Scholastic Inc. Used by permission of the publisher.

"Painting a Picture" by Sandra Liatsos. Copyright ©1992 by Sandra Liatsos. Used by permission of the author.

"Popcorn" from A POEM A DAY by Helen H. Moore. Copyright © 1997 by Helen H. Moore. Used by permission of the author.

"Cloud Parade" from 101 THEMATIC POEMS FOR EMERGENT READERS by Mary Sullivan. Copyright © 1999 by Mary Sullivan. Used by permission of the author.

"Bee" from ANIMAL POEMS FROM A TO Z by Meish Goldish. Copyright © 1994 by Scholastic Inc. Used by permission of the publisher.

"A Magic Chant" from POEMS JUST FOR US by Bobbi Katz. Copyright © 1996 by Bobbi Katz. Used by permission of the author.

"Sweet Dreams" from THE SUPER BOOK OF PHONICS POEMS by Linda B. Ross. Copyright © 2000 by Linda B. Ross. Used by permission of the author.

"Listening" from CARING, SHARING & GETTING ALONG by Betsy Franco. Copyright © 2000 by Betsy Franco. Used by permission of the author.

Edited by Joan Novelli
Cover and interior design by Kathy Massaro
Interior art by Maxie Chambliss, except pages 1, 37, and 64 by Mark Hicks

ISBN: 0-439-26242-9
Copyright © 2004 by Laurie DeAngelis and Rebecca DeAngelis Callan.
All rights reserved.
Printed in the U.S.A.

4 5 6 7 8 9 10   40   11 10 09 08

Contents

A Look Inside This Book

❖ ✳ ❖

An award-winning and favorite author, Tomie dePaola has written books that tell marvelous, heartwarming stories accompanied by watercolor illustrations that stir the imagination. What's more, his books span genres—including fiction, nonfiction, folktale, and wordless picture books. Tomie dePaola's collective works inspire a treasure trove of teaching ideas, from lessons on word families to activities that explore the science of weather and the math behind honeycombs. This book takes a close look at Tomie dePaola classics, with lessons and reproducible activity pages that support the language arts standards. (See page 9.)

The Tomie dePaola books featured in this resource are available at many school and public libraries. And some are likely tucked away in your bookshelves, waiting to be rediscovered! Whether you're using Tomie dePaola titles to build an author study or simply to share a favorite read-aloud, this book has ideas and activities you can turn to again and again. You'll find engaging lessons, interactive reproducible activity pages, ready-to-use graphic organizers, and other great ideas for connecting literature with math, science, and other areas of the curriculum. Here's a sampling of what's inside:

◎ **About Tomie dePaola:** Share this interview with students to help answer their questions about this favorite author.

◎ **Before Reading:** Use the suggestions for introducing each book to teach prediction skills, encourage children to use prior knowledge, build vocabulary, and explore different genres.

◎ **During Reading:** Use the suggestions for each book to take a closer look at such things as text features, picture clues, new vocabulary, and character development.

◎ **After Reading:** From Discussion Starters that reinforce key comprehension skills to extension activities that connect language arts, math, science, movement, and art, these ideas are designed to provide support for the curriculum and motivation for learning.

◎ **Reproducible Activity Pages:** These ready-to-use pages encourage independent learning with games, poetry, writing skill-builders, and other materials.

◎ **Learn More!** In addition to the featured titles, this book includes starter ideas for more favorite books by Tomie dePaola. Use them to inspire your own mini-units for teaching with these favorite books!

Meet Tomie dePaola

Born: September 15, 1934; Meriden, Connecticut
Home: New London, New Hampshire

> 66 It's a dream of mine that one of my books, any book, any picture, will touch the heart of some individual child and change that child's life for the better. 99
>
> —*Tomie dePaola*

Having illustrated more than 200 books and written more than 90, Tomie dePaola (de-POW-la) knows something about ideas. In fact, he's bursting with them. When he's working on one book, he's usually thinking about the next. He's never had writer's block, though he does confess to a single, brief bout with "artist's block." For Tomie, the ideas keep flowing, book after book after book.

Tomie dePaola believes that many people give up on their ideas too easily. He says, "I think if you have an idea, you should hang on to it. Write it down and think about it for a while. Sometimes nothing happens with ideas. But some of them eventually become books."

The important thing about ideas, the prolific dePaola believes, is to explore them. "Ideas are like doors," he says. "It might be a door that gets you to another door. But it might lead you to the secret door that opens up a green meadow outside the castle."

Although Tomie dePaola's books include nonfiction and fiction, he generally draws upon his childhood as a source for inspiration and guidance. An example can be found in his book *The Art Lesson*. Tomie recalls, "*The Art Lesson* is based on something that actually happened. I never forgot that incident. I had been telling that story for years when my editor, Margaret Frith, suggested that it might make a good book. So I sat down and wrote the same story I had been telling."

To create his artwork, dePaola needs to be in his studio, surrounded by his beloved materials. "But," he adds with a laugh, "that's not true for writing. I can write anywhere! I have written drafts of manuscripts on airplanes. It's easy. You just put on your Walkman, flip down the table, and write."

Tomie explains, "I do a first draft that no one sees but me. I do a lot of my writing in my head first, just thinking the story through. Usually, it's a revised second draft that gets typed neatly and sent along to my editor. Then my editor reads it and makes suggestions. We often work on the final draft together. We sit down, side by side, and write together."

Adapted from *The Big Book of Picture-Book Authors & Illustrators*, by James Preller (Scholastic Professional Books, 2001). Photo of Tomie dePaola courtesy of Penguin Putnam, Suki Coughlin.

◆ Tip ◆

Learn more about Tomie dePaola, including his childhood and family, with his Newbery Honor winner *26 Fairmount Avenue* (Putnam, 1999). Other books in the Fairmount Avenue series include *On My Way* (Putnam, 2001), *Here We All Are* (Putnam, 2001), *What a Year!* (Penguin Putnam, 2002), and *Things Will Never Be the Same* (Putnam, 2003). For more information, visit these Web sites:

Internet School Library Media Center
(falcon.jmu.edu/~ramseyil)
Discover tons of terrific biography links, lesson plans, and more at this Web site.

Children's Literature
(www.childrenslit.com)
This Web site is packed with information about authors and illustrators, and includes information on 26 of Tomie dePaola's most famous books.

Activities to Use With Any Tomie dePaola Book

Each of Tomie dePaola's more than 90 stories offers exciting opportunities to enliven lessons in the classroom. The suggestions below may be used with most any Tomie dePaola book to learn more from the story.

Teaching With the Pictures

Strengthen a range of skills with a look at a book's illustrations, beginning with the cover.

Predicting: Examine the book's cover. Before reading the book, invite students to name titles of other books they've read by Tomie dePaola. Ask: "What do you notice about the cover of this book? What does this picture suggest this book might be about? What does Tomie dePaola want us to know before we begin reading?"

Observing: Before reading, encourage students to share observations about what is happening in the pictures, using lots of details. Ask: "What information is the author sharing with us in this illustration?"

Problem-Solving: Use illustrations as support for reading text. Illustrations frequently provide students with insights into the meaning of words they read. After reading the book aloud, discuss ways in which the words are supported by the illustrations. Students may find this strategy helpful, especially when they encounter unfamiliar words.

Exploring the Story

From predicting and sequencing to summarizing and synthesizing, here's how to use the books to build strong reading skills.

Predicting: What might happen next? Encourage students to think about what has happened in the story so far and what could happen next. Ask: "Why does your prediction make sense?" Use the What's Next? reproducible (page 10) to help students develop thoughtful predictions.

Sequencing: Do an instant replay. Invite students to retell the story. This activity not only deepens comprehension but also offers you an opportunity to assess understanding. Note whether each child recalls the story's sequence, including the beginning, middle, and end. Take the retelling process a step further by having children make a flap book. Give each child a sheet of paper. Guide children in following these steps to make the book:

◎ With the paper in a horizontal position, fold it in half from the top down.

◎ Divide the top portion into three flaps by making two cuts as indicated in the illustration. Label the outside of the first flap "Beginning." Label the center flap "Middle" and the last flap "Ending."

◎ On the outside of each flap use words to tell what happens at the beginning, middle, and end of the story. Lift each flap, and draw a picture to go with your words.

Classifying: Explore genre by discussing whether a book is fiction, nonfiction, mystery, poetry, and so on. Ask: "What clues should we look for? Where in the text can we find evidence?"

Organizing Data: Identify characters, plot, setting, and theme. Students can make a story map to show what they learn. To make a map, have students turn a sheet of paper horizontally and make two rows of four or five boxes. They can number the boxes and fill them in with events (in order) from the story. Thinking about characters, plot, setting, and theme will help them choose important details for their story map.

Conflict and Resolution: Will Big Anthony ever get the pasta pot to stop making pasta? Will Strega Nona save the day? Having characters encounter problems is a common plot device. Suspense grows as we turn the pages. Have students use the Pick a Problem reproducible (page 11) to identify the main problem in a story and how it was resolved.

Tip

▲▲▲▲▲▲▲

Students may notice that Tomie dePaola has a distinctive signature that includes a heart shape. According to him, the heart shape is a kind of shorthand for love. Encourage students to create their own artist signature. Some students may be interested in incorporating a particular shape or design into their signature. Invite them to think about what they want their signature to communicate.

Synthesizing: Use the Book Review reproducible (page 12) to encourage reflection and to invite students to form and express opinions about the stories they read. Also see Speech Bubble Responses (below), for a literature response activity that teaches students how to use dialogue in their writing.

Story Quilt

Sharing favorite scenes from a book by making a story quilt is a great way to promote thoughtful discussions and retellings.

◎ Begin by having students brainstorm different scenes from the story. Record each contribution on chart paper.

◎ Determine as a class which scenes help retell the story. Invite students to work in pairs to illustrate the scenes on drawing paper. (Assign scenes to avoid duplication.)

◎ When students have completed their drawings, work together as a class to put the scenes in sequence. It may help to lean the illustrations on the chalkboard ledge during the sequencing process, so that students can see each of the scenes with ease.

◎ Number the scenes, and then place them in a grid format on a bulletin board.

◎ If you have an odd number of scenes, students can develop a title page or table of contents for the story quilt. If you like, add a page with students' signatures.

Speech Bubble Responses

Encourage students to express opinions about what they read, and teach them how to write dialogue with these engaging murals.

◎ Display a long sheet of mural paper. Cut out large speech bubbles for children to write on. Glue these to the paper.

◎ After reviewing how to use quotation marks to write dialogue, let children write their opinion about a story in a speech bubble (including dialogue tags so readers know who is speaking) and attach it to the mural.

◎ Have children draw their pictures next to the speech bubbles. To add color and texture, let students glue colorful yarn around their speech bubbles to outline them.

Connections to the Language Arts Standards

Mid-Continent Research for Education and Learning (McREL), a nationally recognized, nonprofit organization, has compiled and evaluated national and state standards—and proposed what teachers should provide for their students to become proficient in language arts, among other curriculum areas. The reading and writing activities in this book support these standards for grades 1–3 in the following areas:

Uses the general skills and strategies of the reading process and reading skills and strategies to understand and interpret a variety of literary texts:

◆ Uses basic elements of phonetic analysis (for example, common letter-sound relationships and vowel sounds) to decode unknown words

◆ Uses basic elements of structural analysis (for example, compound words and spelling patterns) to decode unknown words

◆ Understands level-appropriate vocabulary

◆ Reads aloud familiar stories, poems, and passages with fluency and expression (for example, rhythm, tone, intonation)

◆ Uses meaning clues (for example, title and cover) to aid comprehension and make predictions about content

◆ Knows main ideas or theme, setting, main characters, main events, sequence, and problems in stories

◆ Makes simple inferences regarding the order of events and possible outcomes

◆ Relates stories to personal experience

Source: Content Knowledge: A Compendium of Standards and Benchmarks for K–12 Education (3rd ed.). *Mid-Continent Research for Education and Learning, 2000. For more information about McREL and to learn more about the topics and benchmarks within each language arts standard, go to the Web site:* **http://mcrel.org**.

Uses the general skills and strategies of the writing process and uses grammatical and mechanical conventions in written compositions:

◆ Uses prewriting strategies to plan written work (for example, discusses ideas with peers)

◆ Uses strategies to organize written work (for example, includes a beginning, middle, and ending; uses sequence of events)

◆ Uses writing and other methods (for example, drawing pictures) to describe familiar persons, places, objects, or experiences

◆ Writes in a variety of forms or genres (for example, picture books, stories, and responses to literature)

◆ Uses conventions of spelling in written compositions (for example, letter-sound relationships)

Uses listening and speaking strategies for different purposes:

◆ Makes contributions in class and group discussions

◆ Asks and responds to questions

◆ Recites and responds to familiar stories, poems, and rhymes with patterns (for example, retells in sequence; relates information to own life; describes character, setting, plot)

◆❋◆ What's Next? ◆❋◆

You have just finished reading a few pages of a book written by Tomie dePaola. Think about what you've read. Fill in the blanks.

◎ **The title of the book is** _____ .

◎ **Here's what's happened so far:**

First _____

_____ .

Then _____

_____ .

◎ **Here's what I think will happen next:**

First _____

_____ .

Then _____

_____ .

This is why: _____

_____ .

Teaching With Favorite Tomie dePaola Books   Scholastic Teaching Resources

◆ ❋ ◆ Pick a Problem ◆ ❋ ◆

◎ **Which Tomie dePaola book did you read?**

Title: _____

◎ **Which character(s) had a problem?**

Name(s): _____

_____

◎ **Describe the problem. Be sure to include details from the book.**

_____

_____

◎ **How was it solved?**

_____

_____

◎ **Explain two other ways the problem could have been solved.**

① _____

_____

② _____

_____

Name _____ Date _____

❖✹❖ Book Review ❖✹❖

What is your opinion of the book you read? Write your answers to the questions below, letting your friends know the inside scoop.

1 **Which Tomie dePaola book did you read?** Title: _____

2 **Who was your favorite character?**

Name: _____

Draw a picture of him or her in the frame.

3 **Why did you like him or her? Explain.**

_____

_____

_____

4 **Did you like reading the book? Why?**

_____

_____

5 **Would you recommend this book to a friend? Why?**

_____

_____

6 **Would you recommend this book to a grown-up? Why?**

_____

_____

7 **Who would not like reading this book? Why?**

_____

_____

Teaching With Favorite Tomie dePaola Books Scholastic Teaching Resources

Watch Out for the Chicken Feet in Your Soup

WATCH OUT FOR THE CHICKEN FEET IN YOUR SOUP

story and pictures by
Tomie dePaola

(SIMON & SCHUSTER, 1974)

When Joey brings a friend to meet his doting grandmother, he's surprised to discover how well his grandmother and friend get along... and how much he, too, values her attention.

Before Reading

Talk with students about the title. Have them predict what this book is about. What kinds of soups have students tried? Has anybody ever had chicken in their soup? How about chicken feet? What uncommon ingredients have students sampled in their soups?

During Reading

Invite students to examine the illustrations and notice the ways in which Joey shows his feelings (embarrassment, anger, appreciation) in the story. For example, on the first page Joey greets his old-fashioned grandmother at the door with open arms. Then on the next page, he cringes when she pinches his face. Encourage children to make connections between events in the story and the way Joey's feelings change.

After Reading

Use these questions to explore the ways in which illustrations can help readers learn more about characters:

◎ How was Joey feeling when Eugene got all of the attention? How do the pictures help you know?

◎ What happens after the bread is baked? How does Joey's expression help you understand how he feels?

◎ What other expressions on characters' faces tell you something about their feelings?

Concepts and Themes

○ Feelings
○ Friendship
○ Families
○ Differences

Arrivederci! (Language Arts)

Joey's grandmother uses Italian words throughout the book. Use them in an activity that reminds students that illustrations usually support text in their books.

◉ Invite students to share words they know in a language other than English. Have fun saying the words together.

◉ Ask children what language Joey's grandmother speaks in the story (*Italian*). Invite students to recall any of the Italian words and phrases she used, such as *mio bambino* (my baby), *zuppa* (soup), *mangia* (eat), and *arrivederci* (goodbye).

◉ Revisit these portions of the story, paying particular attention to the pictures. Let students hunt for clues in the pictures to guess the meaning of the Italian words.

◉ Make a connection to students' own lives by letting them share words they associate with their grandparents (or great-aunts or great-uncles). Are any of the words in a language other than English? How do children know what these words mean?

Baking Bread Dolls (Science, Math)

Create dolls just like Eugene and Joey's grandma made in the story. To start, purchase raw pizza dough from a pizza parlor. (It's also available in the refrigerated aisle of many supermarkets.) To prepare this dough, knead in 1 teaspoon of cinnamon. Or you can make the dough by following Tomie dePaola's grandmother's recipe. You'll find her recipe printed on the last page of *Watch Out for the Chicken Feet in Your Soup*.

Ingredients

● dough

● 1 teaspoon cinnamon

● 2 tablespoons all-purpose flour

● 3 whole eggs (in shells)

● 1/2 teaspoon water

● 1 egg yolk

1 Heat the oven to 350° F.

2 Sprinkle two tablespoons flour on a wide, flat surface and place the dough on it. (A clean, dry table works well.)

3 Divide the dough into three baseball-sized balls and three golf ball-sized balls.

4 Roll the dough balls into ropes, forming three 12-inch ropes and three 8-inch ropes.

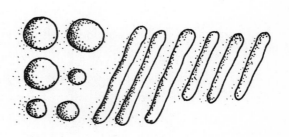

5 Nestle an egg into the end of a short rope of dough. Fold a long rope around the egg so that its ends are nearly even with the short length of dough. Braid the three ropes together, creating what looks like swaddling clothes on an infant. Then repeat the process with the other eggs and lengths of dough.

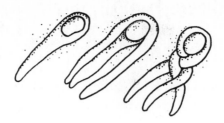

6 Cover the dolls with dishtowels, and let sit for a half hour at room temperature.

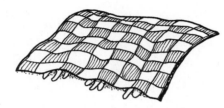

7 Mix 1/2 teaspoon water with the egg yolk. Brush the mixture on the surface of the dough.

8 Bake about 35 minutes or until the dough "is nice and brown."

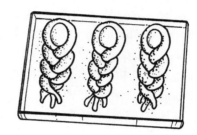

Our Class Cookbook (Writing)

When Eugene visits, he gains insight into the kinds of foods Joey has grown used to—from chicken feet in soup to homemade bread dolls. Invite students to make a collaborative recipe book that helps them share some of the recipes their own families enjoy.

◉ Invite volunteers to describe favorite foods they eat with their families. Give each child a copy of the template on page 17 to take home and fill out with families. Ask students to record information about serving size, ingredients, and directions. Have children use the rest of the space on the page to illustrate the food.

◉ Collect the recipes in a book. To make a cover, write "Our Class Cookbook" on a sheet of paper the same size as the template and invite volunteers to decorate it with related illustrations. Then make a photocopy of the cookbook for each child. Have students punch holes along the left margin and bind the pages together with brass fasteners. Display a copy of the book in your classroom, and send home students' books for families to share and read together.

Book Links

Abuela
by Arthur Dorros
(Dutton, 1991)

A girl, a grandmother, and an imagination take flight in a memorable story that explores ethnic heritage.

The Bag I'm Taking to Grandma's
by Shirley Neitzel
(HarperTrophy, 1998)

This tale about a boy packing for a trip to his grandmother's—and his mother repacking for him—is sure to make every reader smile in recognition.

Wilfrid Gordon McDonald Partridge
by Mem Fox
(Kane/Miller, 1985)

This tender story tells of a boy's attempt to help a senior citizen find her memory.

Chicken Pull-Through (Language Arts)

Build phonological awareness with a pull-through that teaches the consonant digraph *ch-*.

⊚ On a white board or chart paper write the word *chicken*. Invite children to notice the first two letters and the sound they make together.

⊚ Brainstorm other words that start with the same initial sound, the consonant digraph *ch-*. Accept all contributions; however, record only conventional words. Words that begin with *ch-* include: *chunk, chess, cherry, chick, chat, chip, chew, chest, chimp, chill, chase, cheese, chatter, change,* and *choose.*

⊚ Give each child a copy of page 18. Have children cut out the two sections of the pull-through (the chicken and the word strip) along the dashed lines. Help children cut both solid lines on the chicken to create a slit through which they'll pull the word strip.

⊚ Have children thread the word strip though the slits from back to front to back as shown (starting at the bottom of the chicken). Children can line up the word parts next to the letters *ch* and pull on the feet to form and read words!

Tip

▲▲▲▲▲▲▲

In classroom discussions about learning English as a second language, resist the urge to point out second-language learners in your class. If they raise their hand to participate in a discussion about learning English, let them. If they don't, let them participate by simply listening. Being made the center of attention can be both an awkward and frustrating experience for students learning the language of their classmates.

Ears, Eyes, and Hearts

(Language Arts, Social Studies)

Talking with people who speak English as a second language can be challenging for some children. Ask: "How do you think Joey feels about his old-fashioned grandmother using Italian words?" Read this poem with students to further explore the idea of listening. Invite them to think of ways they can kindly listen to someone speaking any language, including listening with their ears, eyes, and hearts.

Listening

I listen mostly with my ears,
but I also listen with my eyes.
I look at your face to see how you feel.
Sometimes it's a surprise.

I listen mostly with my ears;
that's a really good place to start.
But I learn a lot about you
when I listen with my heart.

—Betsy Franco

Our Class Cookbook

**Recipe
Title:** _____

Serves _____ people.

Ingredients: _____   _____

_____   _____

_____   _____

Steps:

1. _____

_____

2. _____

_____

3. _____

_____

4. _____

_____

5. _____

_____

From the kitchen of: _____

Chicken Pull-Through

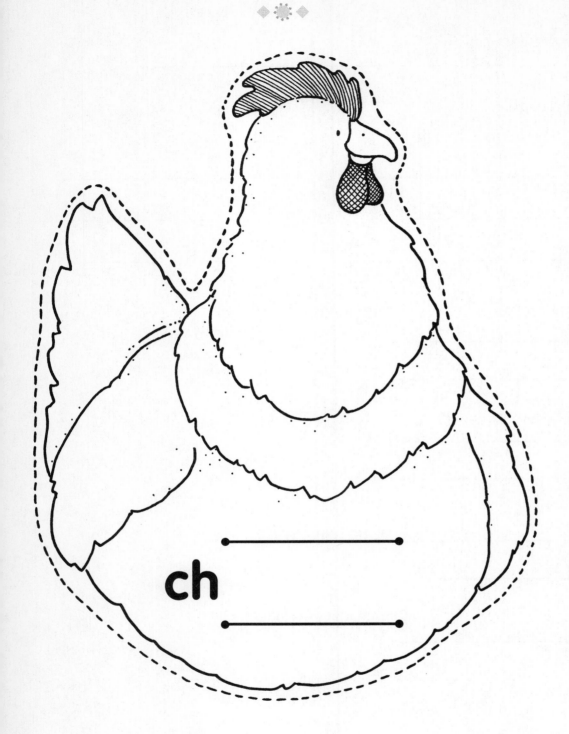

ch ———

ick
ew
unk
at
ip
est
imp
eese
ange

The Cloud Book

(HOLIDAY HOUSE, 1975)

Which kind of cloud looks like cauliflower? This fact-filled book introduces ten common cloud types, making connections to familiar shapes, exploring the weather that comes with them, and sharing the legends that surround them.

Before Reading

Let students describe the cloud pictured on the cover of the book. What kind of weather do they think comes with a cloud like this? Create a KWL chart to record what students know, want to know, and learn about clouds. Begin by dividing a large sheet of tagboard or chart paper into three columns. At the top of the first column write the heading "What We Know About Clouds." At the top of the middle column, write "What We Want to Learn About Clouds." At the top of the third column, write "What We Learned From Reading *The Cloud Book* by Tomie dePaola." Record students' ideas for the first two columns, and then read the book to see what they learn. Place the chart in your science center with a copy of the book. Encourage students to revisit the book and the chart.

During Reading

Notice names for clouds as they are introduced in the book, including *stratus, cumulus, cirrus, cirrocumulus, cirrostratus, altostratus, altocumulus, nimbostratus, stratocumulus,* and *cumulonimbus.* Ask: "Which words end in *stratus? Cumulus?*" Discuss what each ending means in relation to the corresponding cloud.

After Reading

Guide a discussion to draw students' attention to specific facts from the book, comparing them to the kinds of information shared by means of storytelling and legend.

◎ What makes a fact a fact? What are some facts from this story?

◎ In what ways do legends help people understand the natural world? How does this story help explain something about the world?

◎ What are some ways scientists study the weather?

◎ What is something you learned about the weather? (Students can record this on the KWL chart.)

Concepts and Themes

○ Weather
○ Folklore

Tip

You might revisit the text of pages 18 through 20 of *The Cloud Book,* which offers opportunities to discuss specific facts about fog, the meteorological observations of people in the mountains, and the legends of some Native American peoples and the ancient Greeks.

Tip

▲▲▲▲▲▲

Bring newspapers into the weather graphing activity by reading the daily weather forecasts. Examine weather symbols, key words, and map features. There are lots of places to learn more about weather, including these Web sites:

● **teacher.scholastic.com/ lessonplans**

Select "Science" and then "Weather" for lesson plans and activities on climate, air patterns, clouds, and more.

● **www.lib.noaa.gov/ docs/education.html**

The National Oceanic and Atmospheric Administration (NOAA) operates this super site that can be used to connect with lots of other weather-related sites.

Weather Graphs   (Science, Math, Language Arts)

What better way to study weather than by looking out the window? Encourage students to be keen observers of the natural world around them. Use students' observations as a way to discuss weather lore. For example, some people say, "It's raining cats and dogs!" What kind of weather might elicit such a saying? (For more weather sayings and their origins, share *A January Fog Will Freeze a Hog, and Other Weather Folklore*, by Hubert Davis [Random House, 1977].) Record the daily weather on a chart or calendar. At the end of each month, tally the total number of cloudy days, sunny days, and so on. Before you know it, you'll have a year's worth of weather on a chart.

Pop-Up Cloud Books   (Science, Language Arts)

Use the ending of *The Cloud Book* as a beginning for students' own cloud stories. Then use this activity to introduce features of nonfiction text, including the use of diagrams with captions.

◎ Ask: "How could you extend the silly story started at the end of the book? What details would make the story more interesting? What more could we learn about what happened in the beginning, middle, and end of the story?"

◎ Give each child a copy of the sentence strips on page 22, four sheets of blue construction paper, one sheet of white construction paper, and 8 to 12 cotton balls. Students will also need white glue and scissors.

◎ To assemble the books, have students fold a sheet of blue paper in half. Have them cut two 1-inch lines from the fold toward the opening, and then open up the blue paper and "pop" out the cut section to make it three dimensional, like a pop-up book.

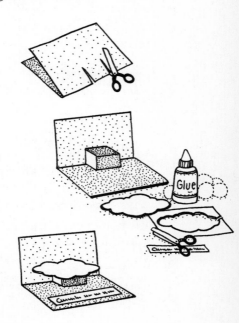

◎ Have students use the white paper to draw and cut out a cloud shape. Have them glue the cloud shape to the pop-out section of the blue paper. They can stretch the cotton ball and glue it to the cloud shape to add details specific to a type of cloud.

◎ Ask students to cut out the cloud sentence that goes with their pop-up cloud and glue it to the bottom of the page.

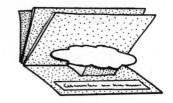

◎ Have students repeat the procedure for each type of cloud. Children can dab gray paint (mixing black and white) on their stratus clouds to suggest rain. Then have them glue the pages back to back, so the book opens from one cloud page to the next.

◎ Show students how to glue the fourth piece of blue paper on as a cover, wrapping it around the folded pages of the book. They can decorate the cover with clouds created from remaining white paper and cotton balls.

Pocket Chart Match-Ups (Language Arts)

Reinforce cloud vocabulary with a pocket chart activity. Photocopy the cloud cards on page 23. Glue to a sheet of tagboard and cut apart the names, pictures, and definitions for each cloud. Mix up the names, definitions, and pictures and place them in a pocket chart. Review difficult vocabulary, such as *atmosphere*. Then invite students to match the words with their definitions and corresponding pictures. They can use the book as a reference and to check their choices. (In order, from top left to right, the pictures are as follows: Altocumulus, Cirrocumulus, Cirrus, Nimbostratus, Cumulus, Stratocumulus, Stratus, Cumulonimbus, Cirrostratus, and Altostratus.) Make individual copies of page 23 for children to use independently. Let them cut apart the pieces and store them in an envelope. Children can take their cloud match-ups home to share with families.

Cloud Parade (Science)

What better way to learn about clouds than by taking a few minutes to watch them drift by? Take students outside to a nearby park or playground and invite them to lie on their backs. Have students close their eyes as you read the poem (right). Then observe the clouds and discuss what you see. Children can make simple cloud "catchers" to enhance their observations. Give each child a large index card. Have children fold the index card in half and cut a window, and then attach a wide craft stick handle. To build science vocabulary, have children decorate their cloud catchers with pictures and labels of different cloud formations.

Book Links

Cloudy With a Chance of Meatballs
by Judi Barrett
(Atheneum, 1978)

What reader could resist an adventure to the town of Chewandswallow, where it rains soup and snows mashed potatoes?

Sun Up, Sun Down
by Gail Gibbons
(Harcourt, 1983)

This book offers an imaginative introduction to the many ways in which the cycles of the sun impact life on Earth.

Weather
by Seymour Simon
(HarperCollins, 1993)

Packed with engaging photographs, this nonfiction book invites readers to learn about all kinds of weather.

Cloud Parade

When I lie on my back
And watch the sky
A cloud parade
Goes drifting by.

Lions and tigers
And elephants too
A dinosaur's playing
A puffy kazoo.

There are dogs and fish
And castles that fade
In my silent, floating
Cloud parade.

—*Mary Sullivan*

Cumulus clouds are fluffy and thick.

Stratus clouds are low in the sky and cover the sky in layers. They give us rain.

Cirrus clouds are thin and feathery. They are high in the sky.

Cumulus clouds are fluffy and thick.

Stratus clouds are low in the sky and cover the sky in layers. They give us rain.

Cirrus clouds are thin and feathery. They are high in the sky.

Teaching With Favorite Tomie dePaola Books

Scholastic Teaching Resources

Altocumulus	Cirrocumulus		
Cirrus	Nimbostratus		
Cumulus	Stratocumulus		
Stratus	Cumulonimbus		
Cirrostratus	Altostratus		

Large, puffy white or gray middle-altitude clouds.	A thin blanket of transparent clouds found a little higher than stratus clouds.
A wispy white cloud found high in the atmosphere.	A cloud layer that blankets the sky and may bring light rain or snow flurries.
A big, puffy white cloud with a flat bottom. It's found low in the atmosphere.	A dark gray layer of clouds low in the atmosphere. These clouds bring rain.
Gray clouds that blanket the sky in layers and bring rain. They are found low in the atmosphere.	Puffy, dark clouds that blanket the sky in winter.
Groups of small, puffy clouds found high in the atmosphere.	Puffy, dark clouds that look like giant cumulus clouds. They may bring rain and thunderstorms.

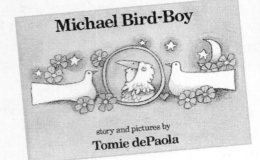

story and pictures by
Tomie dePaola

Michael Bird-Boy

◆ ◆

(PRENTICE HALL, 1975)

Michael lives a happy life in the country until the day the black cloud covers the sky. He seeks out what is causing the cloud and finds the Genuine Shoo-Fly Artificial Honey Factory. This environmental tale depicts Michael convincing the Boss Lady to switch from artificial honey to that produced by real bees.

Concepts and Themes

▲▲▲▲▲▲▲

○ Conservation

○ Science

○ Bees

Before Reading

Invite students to tell what they notice in this book's lovely cover illustration, such as birds, a boy in a bird costume, flowers, stars, and the moon. They may also notice symmetry in the design of the birds, and the author's trademark heart tucked in next to the picture of Michael Bird-Boy. Explore setting by discussing what the picture tells about the time of day. Invite students to list words that describe the feel suggested by this picture—for example, *calm, soft, gentle,* and *peaceful.* Let students predict what this might tell them about the story.

During Reading

Invite students to examine the pictures as you read the book aloud. Call their attention to the scientific details within the illustrations. Follow up with a discussion about how illustrations can help students learn more from what they're reading.

After Reading

Explore story structure with questions that look at problems and solutions.

◎ Why did Michael want to find what was causing the big black cloud?

◎ Why is the Genuine Shoo-Fly Artificial Honey Factory making honey?

◎ How was Michael able to convince Boss Lady that bees should make the honey?

Extending the Book

Honey, Funny, Bee, Whee! (Language Arts)

Strengthen phonemic awareness by inviting students to change beginning sounds of some of the key words in the book. Choose a few key words that are easy for children to rhyme—for example, *honey* and *bee.* While using this strategy to teach phonemic awareness, have children explore all of the consonant combinations with the different rimes. Write the words on fun shapes (such as a bee shape), and have children sort the words into two groups: real words and nonsense words. Discriminating between real and nonsense words is a skill that serves children well as they develop their awareness of the way phonemes sound to the ear.

Sweet Ideas (Science)

Practice organizing data by taking a closer look at honey.

◎ Invite students to brainstorm uses for honey—for example, as a sweetener for baking, to attract insects, and for medicinal purposes.

◎ Make a T-chart to record responses. On one side write the heading "Ways We Eat Honey" and on the other side "Other Ways to Use Honey."

◎ Post the chart where students will have easy access to it. Encourage them to add more ideas to the chart when they have an opportunity.

Extend the Activity Plan a honey tasting party so that all students can appreciate what honeybees give us. (Note: Check for allergies first.) Honey snow cones are fun and easy to make. Just mix one bag of crushed ice and a 12-ounce jar of honey in a bowl and stir. Using an ice cream scoop, serve rounded servings in small cups, or serve smaller portions of several different honeys to let students compare flavors. (Honeybees can use the pollen from almost any flower blossom to create honey, including wildflowers, orange tree blossoms, and clover.)

Math-Magical Honeycombs (Math)

Invite students to put their geometry know-how into action by making honeycombs out of precut paper hexagons.

◎ Give each child a copy of pages 27 and 28.

◎ Ask students to examine the honeycomb template and estimate how many hexagons will fill it. After students have recorded their estimate in the appropriate box on the template page, they can start cutting out hexagons and gluing them to the honeycomb template. Have them count to find out how many hexagons it actually took to fill the template. Compare estimates with the actual number.

◎ Take the geometry connection further by exploring other places students can find a hexagon shape. While most children have seen the hexagon shape of a stop sign, they may not have noticed this shape in many other objects, such as quilts, wood pencil shafts, ceramic floor tiles, bolts, jelly jars, crystals, and gazebos.

Tip

Help visual learners tackle phonemes. Place an alphabet chart near the chalkboard to facilitate sound association. Then invite students to use their rhyming skills to build a list of rhyming words. Your lists may look something like this: *honey (money, sunny, bunny, funny, runny)* or *bee (me, see, tree, flea, flee, sea, key, he, she)*

Book Links

The Earth Is Painted Green: A Garden of Poems About Our Planet
by Barbara Brenner
(Scholastic, 2000)

This collection of poems takes young readers on a lyrical journey through forest and fauna.

The Wump World
by Bill Peet
(Houghton Mifflin, 1970)

This science-fiction story invites children to take a closer look at the natural environment.

Where Once There Was a Wood
by Denise Fleming
(Henry Holt, 2000)

Colorful illustrations and simple text introduce readers to the ways in which people affect animal habitats.

Try these Web sites for fun-to-do projects that connect to themes in *Michael Bird-Boy.*

● **www.honey.com**
Take a trip to The Honey Expert. You'll find honey-related products, recipes, and a history of honey.

● **teacher.scholastic.com/ researchtools/ articlearchives/bugs/ index.htm**
Starting a class research project on bees? This resource page on bugs and insects is a great place to begin.

● **www.pbs.org/wgbh/ nova/bees**
Presented by Nova, this site is a must-see for students eager to learn about the remarkable lives of bees and honey-making. You can even observe bees dancing!

Problems and Solutions (Science)

Michael Bird-Boy might inspire your young environmentalists to investigate problems such as pollution and explore solutions. Plan a research project to encourage environmental awareness and action at a level that is appropriate for students.

◎ Invite children to suggest environmental issues of interest. Encourage attention to local issues, as these will let children make connections in meaningful ways.

◎ Assign each child a topic. Have children find out a little bit about their topic—enough to get an idea about what the problem is. Let children take turns sharing what they find out with the class.

◎ Take a class vote to select an issue for further study, and research it together. Then have students team up to create information pieces about the causes and possible solutions. Brainstorm ways to present information—for example, students might audio- or videotape a 60-second public service announcement, design posters, write letters, or create a computer slide show.

◎ Plan an exhibit for students to share their work with families and others in the school and local community.

Buzzing Bees (Language Arts)

In this poem about a bee, the poet uses the word *buzz* to tickle the reader's ears. Share the poem with students, and invite them to brainstorm other onomatopoeic words (words that imitate the sounds they name), such as *sputter, whir, clang, purr, hush, hum, tick-tock, hiss,* and *cuckoo.* Record students' ideas, and tuck the list in your writing center as a handy reference.

Bee

BUZZ! goes the bee,
Hour after hour,
BUZZ! goes the bee
From flower to flower.

Sucking out the nectar,
Flying it home.
Storing up the nectar,
In the honeycomb!

BUZZ! goes the bee,
Making honey so sweet.
Bee that makes the honey
That I love to eat!

—*Meish Goldish*

Math-Magical Honeycombs

Name _____

Date _____

Estimated Number: _____

Actual Number: _____

Math-Magical Honeycombs

Hexagons

Teaching With Favorite Tomie dePaola Books

Scholastic Teaching Resources

Strega Nona

❖❖

(PRENTICE HALL, 1975)

The Caldecott Honor-winning *Strega Nona* is the first in a series of marvelous tales that tell of life long ago in the region of Calabria, Italy. In this book, Strega Nona teaches Big Anthony about cooking pasta in a magic pot and he learns a lesson about following directions.

Before Reading

Show the cover illustration to students. Remind them that as a class they have examined similar covers by the same author. Ask: "What are some of the images or clues we can look for to be sure it's a book illustrated by Tomie dePaola?" (*There are plants and animals. There's also the heart shape Tomie includes on nearly all of his book covers.*) To get children thinking about character development, invite them to look carefully at the woman pictured on the cover. Ask: "What details do you notice and what might they tell you about this person?" Students' observations may include that the woman is smiling and that she is holding a cauldron and wearing an apron. They may guess from these details that she enjoys cooking.

Concepts and Themes

▲▲▲▲▲▲

○ Responsibility

○ Following directions

○ Cooking

During Reading

While reading, stop occasionally to let students make inferences about the story, and in doing so, to identify with main characters. For example, ask: "How do you imagine Strega Nona feels when she learns Big Anthony tried to use her magic pasta pot?"

After Reading

Use these questions to encourage a lively debate about the characters and events:

◎ What would you do if you had Strega Nona's magic touch?

◎ Would you have helped Big Anthony? How?

◎ Why did Strega Nona warn Big Anthony about the pasta pot? What else could have happened?

◎ What does "the punishment must fit the crime" mean in this story?

◎ Do you agree that Big Anthony should be punished? Why?

◎ What could the townspeople have done to help Big Anthony solve the problem?

Use creative dramatics to further explore plot and character. Students can color and cut out construction paper characters and then glue them to craft sticks to make simple puppets. Or let students script a retelling for a Readers Theater production. Both dramatizations make excellent assessment tools.

Extending the Book

Pocket Chart Sequencing (Language Arts)

This story's sequence of events makes it especially fun to retell. Strengthen sequencing and oral language skills with this pocket chart retelling that spotlights key plot points, including Strega Nona's hiring Big Anthony, his making pasta with the magic pot while Strega Nona was away, the pasta overflowing and endangering the town, Strega Nona's return, and Big Anthony's punishment.

◉ Invite students to brainstorm events that took place in the story. Record each event on chart paper, giving each event its own line.

◉ Cut out each line, creating strips that will fit into your pocket chart.

◉ Discuss the story and ask, "What happened first? Second? Third? Last?" Let students place the strips in order on the pocket chart to retell the story.

◉ Compare the pocket chart retelling with the actual book. Discuss similarities and differences. Are there any additional events students would like to include?

◉ Let students use the sentence strips to retell the story on their own or with a classmate.

One Ziti, Two Fusilli (Math)

Use pasta as math manipulatives! Gather a variety of uncooked pasta shapes (at least three). Begin by discussing what students know about patterns. The simple ABAB, ABBAABBA, and ABCABC patterns may be familiar. Invite students to make a pattern with the different varieties of pasta. They can arrange the shapes first, and then glue them in place on paper when they are satisfied with their work. Have students label or describe their patterns. To extend their skills, invite students to team up and make patterns for one another to extend. Have students record their names and patterns on a sheet of paper. Use this as an opportunity to check students' understanding of this algebra skill.

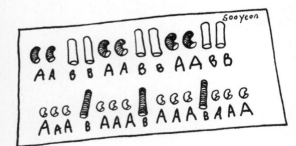

Magic Potion Recipes (Language Arts)

Invite students to write magic potion recipes on 3- by 5-inch cards. Have them write names for their recipes at the top of their cards. Place the cards and a recipe box at a language arts center. Let children visit the center to enjoy reading the recipes. They can practice alphabetizing skills, too, as they file away each recipe using the A to Z dividers as a guide for following alphabetical order.

Linguine Stories (Language Arts)

Display a large black pot or cauldron on a bulletin board as a prop for an activity that invites students to develop alternate endings, explore plot, create additional characters, and so on.

◎ Begin by cutting a large pasta pot from black paper. Attach it to the center of a bulletin board. Add red and orange cellophane "flames" under the pot.

◎ Ask children to brainstorm ideas for a story that features a magic pot. Agree on a beginning and write it on a long linguine-like length of adding machine tape. Invite one child at a time to add on to the story, writing each sentence on a separate length of adding machine tape "linguine." Number the sentences as they are written so that children may sequence them later with ease. When students have finished their story, invite them to tack it up in order on the bulletin board. Reread it as a class.

◎ With students' storytelling skills warmed up, let them write their own linguine stories. Using the adding machine tape noodles puts a fun twist on the writing activity. To spice things up a bit, set a kitchen timer for ten minutes or so. *Tic, tic, tic, bzzz*! Students will love the suspense! Return to the activity several days in a row, each time setting the timer for about ten minutes. Encourage students to use the time to revise their writing, create final drafts, and illustrate.

◎ Replace the first story with the new stories for a potful of reading fun!

Pasta All Over the Place (Art, Language Arts)

Make pasta pictures that highlight problems in the story, reinforce a problem-solution story structure, and strengthen comprehension.

◎ Introduce this activity by leading a discussion about what happened when the pasta wouldn't stop coming out of the magic pot.

◎ Give each child a copy of the Pick a Problem record sheet (page 11). Have students answer the questions, focusing on the problem of the overflowing pasta. As a class, discuss some of the ways the townsfolk, Big Anthony, and Strega Nona could have solved the pasta problem.

◎ Provide students with markers, dried pasta, glue, and construction paper. Have children draw a scene that illustrates the problem and then glue on real pasta for effect.

◎ When the glue on their pictures is dry, let students share their scenes and explain what's happening in their pictures. Some children may talk about the problem the townsfolk faced—mountains of pasta. Others may choose to show the pasta overflowing from Strega Nona's magic pot.

Pasta Poetry (Language Arts)

The author of the poem on page 37 advises the reader to be sure to say the chant "absolutely right." Give each child a copy of page 37. Together, read the poem aloud. Invite students to emphasize the initial letter sounds as they read, articulating clearly. For added fun, you might give children a playful warning about incantations, telling them that if a person doesn't say the words just right, the chant won't work! Follow up by comparing this poem with the chant Strega Nona uses. Ask: "How are they similar? Different?" Write a new magical chant together on chart paper. Try including some rhyming nonsense words and silly images like Bobbi Katz did in this imaginative poem.

Mangiamo Pasta! Let's Eat Pasta! (Math, Language Arts)

Learn about the history of pasta-making by preparing delicious pasta! Begin by inviting students to research the origins of pasta. For example, they might be surprised to learn that since the Chinese first began making pasta in 5,000 B.C.E., more than 600 shapes of pasta have been created around the world! The Italians named the noodles "pasta," which refers to the paste of flour and water with which they're made. To kick off your study of pasta, get some *pasta fresca* from the store or make your own in about 45 minutes. Here is an easy-to-make recipe that serves 8 to 12 adults or a roomful of children:

1 Put four cups of flour in the mixing bowl. Add one egg and stir. Continue adding one egg at a time and stirring to make the dough.

2 Sprinkle 2 tablespoons flour onto a clean, dry table and place the dough on it. Knead the dough to make a ball of smooth, firm dough.

3 Roll the dough into a loaf shape, cover with a towel, and let sit for half an hour at room temperature. (Consider rereading *Strega Nona* during this time.)

4 Cut the dough into eight equal slices. Remove one to work with and leave the other seven to sit, covered with the towel.

5 Sprinkle 1 tablespoon flour on the surface of the dough; sprinkle another tablespoon on the surface of the table and on the rolling pin. Roll out the dough, dust it with flour, and fold it into thirds. Repeat this step four times, rolling out the dough, flouring, and folding it each time.

6 At this point you can cut the pasta by hand. If you have access to several garlic presses, break dough into olive-sized pieces, place each inside a garlic press, and let children squeeze to form short, wide pieces of spaghetti. Or, if a pasta machine is available, select the pasta style you'd like to cut on the machine and feed the pasta through. Repeat steps five and six until all the pasta is rolled, cut, and ready to cook. Cook in a pot of boiling water. (NOTE: Most styles of fresh pasta take only a minute or two to cook.)

Pasta Ingredients

- 4 cups all-purpose flour (for the dough)

- 1 cup all-purpose flour (for kneading and working with the dough)

- 6 eggs

Learn More With the Strega Nona Series

Team *Strega Nona* with other books in this series for a mini-unit that explores character development, setting, plot structure, and more. Other titles in the series are *Strega Nona's Magic Lessons* (Harcourt Brace, 1982); *Midwest Strega Nona* (Turtleback, 1986); *Merry Christmas, Strega Nona* (Harcourt Brace, 1991); *Strega Nona Meets Her Match* (Putnam, 1993); *Strega Nona: Her Story* (Putnam, 1996); *Strega Nona Takes a Vacation* (Putnam, 2000); and the Big Anthony books: *Big Anthony and the Magic Ring* (Harcourt Brace, 1979) and *Big Anthony: His Story* (Putnam, 1998). Activities to use with this series follow.

What If? Webs (Language Arts)

Use this activity to explore plot development and the way a decision made by a character sets the story's conflict in motion. For example, in *Strega Nona*, Big Anthony ignores Strega Nona's warning about the pasta pot and decides to make pasta on his own. And what a mess he makes! In *Strega Nona Meets Her Match*, Strega Nona ignores Strega Amelia's new business at the bottom of the hill and decides to continue life as usual. And Strega Nona ends up with no customers!

◎ After reading a Strega Nona story, make a What If? web on chart paper, writing the title of the book at the top. Draw a circle at the center and write a question that begins with "What if…" For example, after reading *Strega Nona* you might ask, "What if Big Anthony hadn't bragged to the town that he'd seen Strega Nona use a magic pot?" After reading *Strega Nona Takes a Vacation*, you might ask, "What if Bambolona hadn't switched the presents?"

◎ Invite students to take turns answering the question to explore different turns the plot might have taken. Record each idea on the web.

◎ Repeat the activity with other Strega Nona books. Compare different characters' decisions and the conflicts that resulted.

Character Cutouts (Language Arts)

Explore character traits by making life-sized cutouts of Strega Nona, Bambolona, and Big Anthony.

◎ Divide the class into three groups: a Strega Nona group, a Bambolona group, and a Big Anthony group.

◎ Have each group make a character silhouette, tracing the body outline of a volunteer on large sheets of craft paper. Provide students with construction paper, scissors, glue, and other art supplies. (Cloth and yarn are a fun addition for this activity.) Invite groups to refer to illustrations in the Strega Nona books as they "dress" and add details to their group's character. Allow the projects to dry flat overnight.

◎ Have children record the character's name and three traits on the cutout. For each trait, have the group cite evidence from two Strega Nona books. You may want to provide a graphic organizer such as the one on page 38 for students to use as a guide.

A Trip to Calabria, Italy
(Social Studies)

Introduce this activity by taking students on a virtual field trip to Italy! Preselect Web sites for children to view. Look for those that show photographs and give descriptions of this region's geographic characteristics, such as the mountains and sea. Let students draw maps of the Strega Nona stories' settings to show what they learn. Before students get started, help them think about what they already know about Calabria by asking: "What have we learned about this region from Tomie dePaola's illustrations?" Encourage children to refer to the illustrations in the Strega Nona series to discover whatever they can about geographical features such as the rolling hills, cypress trees, and the walled village. Have students draw arrows on their maps to indicate key places from the stories, including the little house on the hill where Strega Nona lives, the fountain in the middle of the town square, Bambolona's father's bakery, and so on. To take mapping skills further, challenge children to draw the whereabouts of Grandma Concetta's house (at the seashore) and the town where Big Anthony moved from (to the North).

The Strega Nona Game
(Language Arts, Social Studies)

Playing games is a terrific way to learn and have fun at the same time. Celebrate the Strega Nona books with a board game that reinforces an understanding of story elements and provides problem-solving practice. Make several copies of the game for the classroom, as the game may be played in small groups or at a learning center.

Begin by making photocopies of the game board on pages 40–41 and the game cards on page 39. Glue the game board patterns together where indicated. Have children color the game boards and cut apart the game cards. You may want to mount both the game boards and game cards on tagboard and laminate for durability. Finally, make dice by cutting a sponge into cubes. Mark dots on each side. For this game, you'll need one to four dots on each side. (Too many dots will make the game go too fast.)

Before play, introduce the elements and purpose of the game. Explain that children take turns rolling a die, answering fun trivia questions about Strega Nona books, and moving playing pieces forward on the game board. Demonstrate how to hold the card so that other players cannot see it, and point out where a child can find the answers on each playing card. When students are ready to play, provide each group with a game board, set of game cards, and number die. Children may use colorful plastic bingo chips or different shapes of pasta as playing pieces.

How to Play

1 Each player chooses a game marker and puts his or her marker on the Start space.

2 A volunteer stacks the game cards facedown and places them beside the game board.

3 Each player rolls the number die. The child with the highest number goes first. Then students take turns in clockwise order.

4 The first player rolls the die and moves his or her playing piece the number of spaces shown on the top of the die. The player's piece may land on a square that says "Answer a Question!" It may also land on a square with specific directions, such as "Strega Amelia comes to visit. Go back one." If the piece lands on a square that indicates a question, the child to the player's left takes on the role of Reader. The Reader selects a playing card from the top of the deck and reads it to the player. If the player answers the trivia question correctly, he or she may advance one space on the game board. If the player does not answer correctly, his or her game piece stays put and the Reader reads the correct answer aloud. Play continues with the next child.

5 Players continue rolling the die and moving their markers until they've all reached the End space.

Enchanted Objects (Language Arts, Writing)

Combine the excitement of magic with a love of Strega Nona by turning ordinary shoe boxes into containers for enchanted objects.

◎ Begin by asking volunteers to answer the following questions: "How would you feel if you had a magical item like Strega Nona's pasta pot or her gold ring? What would your object be? What magical characteristics would it have?"

◎ Explain that children will be selecting three objects and placing them in a box. Each item should have a special significance to children, as Strega Nona's magic pot had to her. The items, such as favorite toys, books, or articles of clothing, are then infused with magical properties. One child may choose a baseball glove that, when put on, gives the wearer the miraculous ability to catch any fastball. Another child may select a soft hairbrush that, when used regularly, relieves the user of any worries.

◎ Give each child three index cards. Ask students to write an explanation about why they chose each item for the box, how it may be used, and

If you liked teaching with **Strega Nona**, you may enjoy reading more books about Big Anthony's adventures in Calabria. Read **Big Anthony: His Story** (Putnam, 1998); **Big Anthony and the Magic Ring** (Harcourt Brace, 1987); and **Tony's Bread** (Putnam, 1989).

any special words or chants needed to make it work. Here's an example of what a child may write about a pair of sandals: *This old pair of sandals is my favorite pair of shoes. I wear them every summer, even though they're too small. Whenever I put them on, they instantly bring me to my cousin Tina's beach house. To make their magic work, I have to say, "Sandy Toes, Sandy Toes, Where I'll go . . . only Tina knows."*

Strega Says (Language Arts)

This playful twist on a favorite game (Simon Says) is sure to be a big hit with the Strega Nona fans in your classroom, who will love pretending to be the colorful characters from the stories. To play the game, choose one child to be the caller, who is identified as the Strega. The rest of the children, or players, stand in a row facing the Strega, who in turn tells them what character they need to behave like to stay in the game. But here's the catch! Each of the Strega's instructions needs to be preceded by the phrase "Strega says." For example, if the caller announces, "Strega says . . . clean the windows like Big Anthony," each player must pretend to wash windows. Any player who doesn't make a window-washing motion with his or her hands is out, and needs to step back from the row of players. If, for example, the caller doesn't begin his or her instruction with the phrase "Strega says," the players may not move their bodies at all. Any player that does move is out, and needs to step back from the row. The game continues with the caller announcing instructions and the players pretending to be different characters from the stories—dancing the tarantella like Handsome Big Anthony, walking and carrying loaves of bread on their heads like Bambolona, blowing three kisses to the pasta pot like Strega Nona, and so on. When there is just one player left in the row, he or she replaces the Strega and a new game begins.

A Magic Chant

Mumbo
jumbo
griggle
grumbo!
Fista
fasta
lasta
pasta!
Joga
voga
foga
VOO!
Ickle
pickle
parsley stew!

Say these words by day or night.
Get them absolutely right.
Learn them and you'll be prepared
For anything that makes you scared.

Mumbo
jumbo
griggle
grumbo!
Fista
fasta
lasta
pasta!
Joga
voga
foga
VOO!
Ickle
pickle
parsley stew!

—Bobbi Katz

Character
Cutouts

◆ ✳ ◆

Character's Name:

_____

Trait:

_____

_____

_____

Title: _____

_____

Evidence: _____

_____

_____

_____

_____

Title: _____

_____

Evidence: _____

_____

_____

_____

_____

Teaching With Favorite Tomie dePaola Books   Scholastic Teaching Resources

Strega Nona
❖ ✳ ❖
Game

....

Game Cards

Q. **What gifts did Strega Nona send from the seashore?**

A. Answers may include: candy and bubble bath

(Strega Nona Takes a Vacation)

Q. **Who did Strega Nona visit on vacation?**

A. Grandma Concetta at her house on the seashore

(Strega Nona Takes a Vacation)

Q. **What happens when Strega Nona puts on her golden ring?**

A. She turns into a beautiful lady, in fancy clothes.

(Big Anthony and the Magic Ring)

Q. **What happens when Big Anthony puts on Strega Nona's golden ring?**

A. Answers may include: He turns into an irresistibly handsome man. The ladies in the village don't let him stop dancing. The ladies chase him into the countryside.

(Big Anthony and the Magic Ring)

Q. **Why did Big Anthony apply for a job at the little house on the hill?**

A. Answers may include: He didn't pay attention. His other jobs didn't work out. He saw a sign for someone who needed a helper.

(Big Anthony: His Story)

Q. **What happened when Strega Amelia left Big Anthony in charge?**

A. Answers may include: He used her modern machines the wrong way. He mixed up the magic creams. He made the townspeople want to return to Strega Nona's services.

(Strega Nona)

Q. **How does Strega Nona stop the pasta from boiling?**

A. With a magic song and three kisses.

(Strega Nona)

Q. **Where does Strega Nona live?**

A. In the region of Calabria, Italy

(Strega Nona)

Q. **Who is Strega Nona's helper?**

A. Big Anthony

(Strega Nona)

Q. **Who does Strega Nona train to be a Strega?**

A. Bambolona

(Strega Nona's Magic Lessons)

Q. **Who taught Strega Nona to be a Strega?**

A. Grandma Concetta

(Strega Nona: Her Story)

Q. **Who is Strega Nona's childhood friend?**

A. Strega Amelia

(Strega Nona: Her Story)

Q. **Who is Bambolona's father?**

A. The baker

(Strega Nona's Magic Lessons)

Q. **Why can't Big Anthony be a Strega?**

A. He is a boy. Boys can't be Stregas.

(Strega Nona's Magic Lessons)

Q. **Who did Big Anthony work for in Calabria?**

A. The baker

(Strega Nona's Magic Lessons)

Q. **What is one animal that Tomie dePaola includes in his illustrations?**

A. Answers may include: goat, bird, rabbit, cat

(The Strega Nona series)

Q. **What is Strega Nona's most treasured possession?**

A. Her pasta pot

(Strega Nona)

Q. **What is Strega Nona's native language?**

A. Italian

(The Strega Nona series)

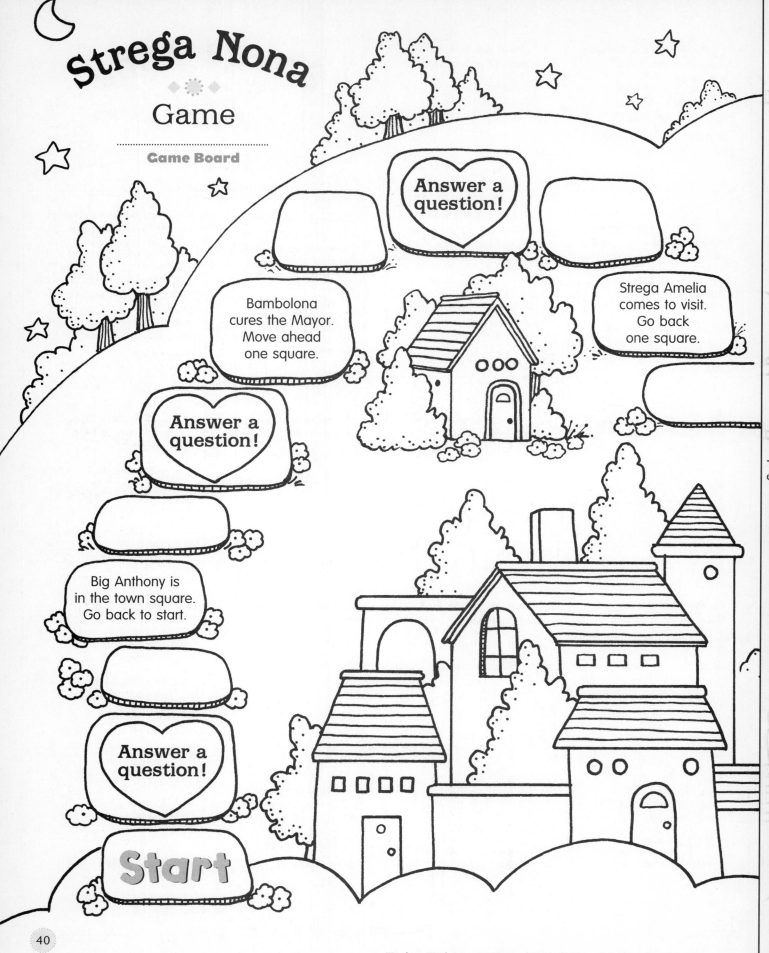

Strega Nona

Game

Answer a question!

Bambolona cures the Mayor. Move ahead one square.

Strega Amelia comes to visit. Go back one square.

Answer a question!

Big Anthony is in the town square. Go back to start.

Answer a question!

Start

40

Answer a question!

Finish

Big Anthony surprises Strega Nona. Free roll.

Bambolona makes a successful love potion. Move ahead two squares.

Answer a question!

Answer a question!

Big Anthony has to eat all the pasta he made by accident. Lose a turn.

Big Anthony turns Strega Nona into a toad. Go back one square.

Answer a question!

Teaching With Favorite Tomie dePaola Books   Scholastic Teaching Resources

The Popcorn Book

(HOLIDAY HOUSE, 1978)

Twin boys Tony and Tiny tell this story about making popcorn. Tony makes the popcorn while Tiny shares the information he discovers about popcorn and its origin.

Concepts and Themes

- Science
- Legends
- Food

Before Reading

Introduce the topic of this book (popcorn) with an activity that combines graphing and classifying skills. Make a simple "Favorites" graph to show various ways of preparing corn (on the cob, creamed, popped, in soup, and so on). Give each child a graph marker (a piece of popcorn would be fun). Let children take turns telling their favorite way to enjoy corn and placing their graph marker in the appropriate column. (Include an "I don't like corn" option on the graph.) Discuss results: "Which way do most children enjoy corn?"

Use a KWL chart to set up a framework for understanding the nonfiction information included in this story. Complete the first two sections (What I Know, What I Want to Know) before reading.

During Reading

Some students may have experience reading literature with speech bubbles; others may not. Pause from time to time in order to draw attention to the speech bubbles in this story. Point out that one twin in the story is talking about history and the other is talking about following the steps to make popcorn.

After Reading

Use the story to explore text features and the way authors weave facts into fiction.

- Strengthen print awareness by drawing attention to the differences in the text within the speech bubbles. Ask: "Why do you think there is one kind of print in this speech bubble [point to one with standard print] and a different kind in this speech bubble [point to one with uppercase letters]? Guide students to understand that this text feature helps readers know who in the story is talking. Invite students to discuss other ways to figure out which twin is talking.

- Did students learn anything new about popcorn? Complete the third section of the KWL chart (What We Learned). Use the class discussion as an opportunity to assess comprehension.

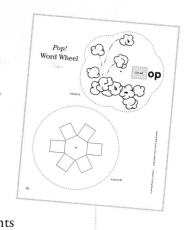

Pop! **Word Wheel** (Language Arts)

Build vocabulary for the *-op* word family with this word wheel.

- Photocopy a class set of page 46. (Use heavy paper for durability, or glue the copies to tagboard to reinforce.) Give one copy to each student.

- On wheel B, in the boxes, have students write the letters for beginning sounds of words that end in *-op*. Guide students in writing the letters as shown on the illustration, right. (Or add these in advance of photocopying the page.) Letters may include: *ch, sh, t, st, dr, fl, m, h,* and *p.* You may find it helpful to first review this word family with students and set up a word wall for reference.

- Have students cut out each wheel. Guide students in cutting out the window on wheel A, placing wheel A on B, and attaching the wheels at the center with a brass fastener.

- Demonstrate how the wheels move. Then invite students to read their *-op* family words and to think of even more words they could add to their popcorn wheel.

POP! (Movement, Math)

These kinesthetic and counting activities add a playful touch to lessons while letting students use their imagination.

- **First, You Sizzle!** Have children squat, pretending to be corn kernels sitting in the oil at the bottom of a pan. As the oil starts to heat up and sizzle, children rock slowly. As oil continues to heat, they rock faster and faster until finally . . . POP! Students pop up to a standing position and stretch their hands above their heads. They've popped!

- **1, 2, 3, 4, Pop!** Gather children in a circle. Have them count off, starting with 1, and then 2, 3, and 4. The fifth person says "POP!" and pops up in the circle. Repeat, until the counting and popping has gone all the way around the circle. As a variation, count by twos (2, 4, 6, 8, POP!), tens (10, 20, 30, 40, POP!), ordinals (first, second, third, fourth, POP!), and so on.

Tip

▲▲▲▲▲▲

Try playing 1, 2, 3, 4, POP! in different languages:

French: un, deux, trois, quatre, POP!

Spanish: uno, dos, tres, quatro, POP!

Japanese: ichi, ni, san, chi, POP!

Italian: uno, due, tre, quattro, POP!

Tip

▲▲▲▲▲▲

Before beginning the activity, you may want to invite children to revisit the story with a classmate. Often it's the retelling of a story that triggers memories and deepens understandings.

Book Links

Corn Is Maize:
The Gift of the Indians
by Aliki
(HarperTrophy, 1986)

Young readers can learn something new about corn in a nonfiction picture book that tells where corn came from, how it's milled, how it's used, and more.

Popcorn
by Alex Moran
(Green Light Readers, 2003)

Catchy rhymes and lively illustrations tell the story of what happens when there's too much popcorn in the pot.

The Popcorn Shop
by Alice Low
(Cartwheel Books, 1994)

What happens when a popcorn machine pops day and night? Find out in this rhyming Hello Reader book.

Corncob Collages (Science, Language Arts, Art)

Show students an ear of corn. Invite them to touch it, feeling the texture of the husk and the corn kernels. What do they know about the husk? The kernels? The cob? Revisit the KWL chart to remind students how much they already knew about corn and how much they learned from *The Popcorn Book*. Then let them use an ear of corn as a model for making an informative and fun display.

◎ Divide the class into small groups. Give each group an ear of corn. Let children look closely at the corn, peeling away a bit of the husk to see inside.

◎ Give each child a sheet of 12- by 18-inch white paper, some unpopped popcorn, and an index card. Make available glue and different shades of green paper or tissue paper.

◎ Have children draw or trace the ear of corn on their paper, paint the inside with glue, and cover it with the unpopped popcorn. They can tear husk shapes from the green paper and glue them along the corncob shape.

◎ Ask children to write a favorite popcorn fact on the index card and glue it to the paper.

◎ Arrange corncob collages and facts on a bulletin board to create a colorful, fact-filled display. As children visit the display, they can review and celebrate all of the facts they've learned. What a great way to revisit the information in the book!

Indians wore popcorn as jewelry.

They found popcorn in a cave that was 5,600 years old.

Corn Crop (Science, Language Arts)

This easy science experiment lets children use prediction, observation, and other science process skills.

◎ Fold a damp paper towel and place it around the inside of a clear jar. Pour enough lukewarm water in the jar to cover the bottom. (This will help the paper towel stay damp.)

◎ Position several unpopped popcorn kernels in between the side of the jar and the paper towel. Invite students to predict what will happen. Record predictions in a class journal.

◎ As a class, revisit predictions and record observations one hour later, two hours later, the next day, and so on. (Germination will probably occur within three days.) Discuss observations and results, teaching key vocabulary in the process, such as *germination*, *root hairs*, *roots*, *stem*, *stalk*, *leaves*, *flower*, and *kernel*.

Tip

For more prediction fun, experiment with placing some kernels in a dish with hot water and others in a dish with cold water. Or place some in a sunny windowsill and some away from sunlight. Compare results.

Popcorn Poetry (Language Arts)

The repeated words *pop* and *popcorn* make this poem especially fun to read. Before reading the poem aloud to students, ask them to make the sound the letter *p* represents. Ask them to make this sound whenever they hear you say the word *pop* or *popcorn*. By the time you've finished reading the poem, your students will almost be able to smell the popcorn!

Popcorn

Pop, pop, popcorn,
popping in the pot!
Pop, pop, popcorn,
eat it while it's hot!

Pop, pop, popcorn,
butter on the top!
When I eat popcorn,
I can't stop!

—*Helen H. Moore*

Pop!
Word Wheel

◆ ✳ ◆

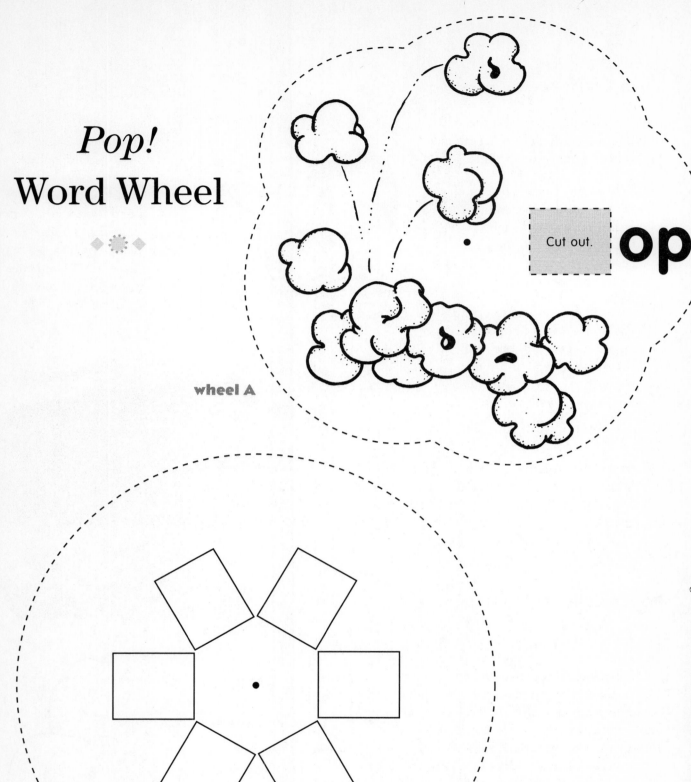

Cut out. **op**

wheel A

wheel B

Teaching With Favorite Tomie dePaola Books   Scholastic Teaching Resources

The Legend of the Bluebonnet

(PUTNAM, 1983)

A Native American girl gives up her most precious possession to help her people in this origin tale of the Texas bluebonnet flower.

Before Reading

Draw attention to the word *legend* in the title. Invite students to share what they think this word means. Read the line on the cover, "retold and illustrated by Tomie dePaola." Ask students what it means that this story is "retold." Guide students to understand that legends, such as Robin Hood and Johnny Appleseed, are stories that are handed down over time by word of mouth. These stories often begin with a small bit of truth, which may be exaggerated or embellished. Let students guess who might have told *The Legend of the Bluebonnet* before, based on what they see on the cover.

During Reading

Call attention to the placement of characters in the story. For example, the illustrations from the beginning of the story show She-Who-Is-Alone as separate from the rest of the Comanche people. The illustrations at the end of the story show her joined by the rest of the tribe. What might Tomie dePaola be trying to tell us without using words?

After Reading

Explore the role of names in the story, examining how the main character's name reflects her position among her people, and the fact that a blue jay is named "the bird who cries 'Jay-jay-jay'."

◎ Why is the main character called She-Who-Is-Alone?

◎ Why is her name changed to One-Who-Dearly-Loved-Her-People?

◎ Why do you think people are often given first, middle, and last names?

◎ What can names tell us about someone?

Concepts and Themes

▲▲▲▲▲▲

○ Sharing

○ Kindness

○ Flowers

○ Legends

Looking at Letters (Language Arts)

Throughout the book, students may notice many capitalized words, including: *Earth*, *Home of the Winds*, *People*, and *Great Spirits*. Use these words as a springboard to a lesson on capitalization. Ask students what words they know that have capital letters—for example, their names. Look around the room for other examples. List the words on chart paper. Sort them into groups by categories, such as Names, Places, and Titles. Review rules for capitalization. Discuss whether the words capitalized in the story fit these rules. (Explain that sometimes authors choose to capitalize words that would not ordinarily be capitalized.) Let children work in small groups to write in their own words a rule that goes with each group of capital-letter words. Display the rules on posters to create a handy classroom writing reference.

Stepping Into a Character's Shoes (Language Arts)

Explore how authors develop characters on the outside and on the inside.

◎ Ask students to offer descriptions of She-Who-Is-Alone. Record their comments on chart paper.

◎ Set up a two-column chart with the headings "On the Outside" and "On the Inside." Have students sort their descriptions of the character into each column.

◎ Revisit the story to allow students to find evidence in the text and illustrations in the story to support their descriptions. What other descriptions can they add? Encourage students to draw inferences based on events to learn more. For example, have students consider how She-Who-Is-Alone felt about losing her doll.

◎ To make connections to students' lives, invite them to discuss with their families something that is not worth a lot of money but that is priceless. Ask students to draw a picture and write or dictate a story about this family treasure. In class, discuss why those items are special and how it would feel to not have them anymore.

The Legend of Old Befana
by Tomie dePaola
(Harcourt Brace Javonovich, 1980)

An old woman's misfortune turns into the good fortune of children around the world on the Feast of the Three Kings.

Miss Rumphius
by Barbara Cooney
(Viking, 1985)

A woman pursues a childhood dream and adds beauty to the world around her.

William's Doll
by Charlotte Zolotow
(Harper & Row, 1972)

In this refreshing tale, a young boy wants just one thing…a doll.

Tip

Read this story at Thanksgiving time. The themes of sharing during famine and remembering the past are a perfect way to recall the first feasts of this country.

The Legend of the Indian Paintbrush

(PUTNAM, 1988)

Little Gopher, a Native American boy, is inspired by the colors of the sunset and discovers his artistic gifts. In the process, he learns of his destiny within the tribe.

Before Reading

If students have already read *The Legend of the Bluebonnet* (see page 47), invite them to use what they learned about that story to guess what kind of story this one is. Continue the discussion about legends, again referring children to the words on the cover "retold and illustrated by Tomie dePaola." Review the meaning of the word *legend*, and let children guess who might have told this story before, based on what they see on the cover.

During Reading

Many of the words in this story are names for abstract ideas, such as *Dream-Vision, Shaman, deeds,* and *faithfulness*. Use these words to reinforce strategies for learning the meaning of unfamiliar words. Begin by writing the words on chart paper. Reread each corresponding portion of the text and look at any supporting illustrations. Ask students to share what they think each word means and how they know. For example, a child might guess what *faithfulness* means based on looking at a familiar word part, *faith*. Other strategies include:

◎ Skip the unfamiliar word and read on. Does a clue pop up?

◎ Ask yourself: "What other word would make sense in this sentence?"

◎ Look at the picture. What information about the story does it show?

After Reading

Explore character development with questions that look at how Little Gopher feels, what he thinks, and what he does.

◎ On the first page of the story, readers learn that Little Gopher can't keep up with the other boys. The illustration doesn't show his face, but what expression do you think he might have in this picture? Why?

◎ When Little Gopher returns to the circle of the People after the Dream-Vision, what do you suppose he is thinking? What are some clues?

◎ Why does Little Gopher leave the pure white buckskin empty for many months? What do you learn about him from this?

Concepts and Themes

○ Legends

○ Family

○ Dreams

Extending the Book

Legend Organizer (Language Arts)

The Indian paintbrush was a source of inspiration for Native Americans, as is much of the natural world. Invite students to think about why the legend of the Indian paintbrush came about. There is an author's note at the end of the book that provides readers with insights about the Texan flower with the same name. Read it with students and discuss. Brainstorm other elements of the natural world, such as rainbows, clouds, the sun, moon, wind, fire, seasons, snow, and tornadoes. Invite students to come up with their own ideas about the origin of each. Provide students with the graphic organizer on page 52 to help organize original legends of their own.

Painting a Story (Science and Language Arts)

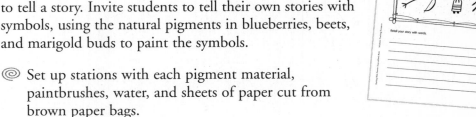

Little Gopher uses berries, soil, and other natural pigments to mix colors for his paint. He paints symbols on buckskin to tell a story. Invite students to tell their own stories with symbols, using the natural pigments in blueberries, beets, and marigold buds to paint the symbols.

◉ Set up stations with each pigment material, paintbrushes, water, and sheets of paper cut from brown paper bags.

◉ Let children crumple the paper to create a crinkled effect. Then have them experiment with using the berries, beets, and buds to paint (on scrap paper first). What's the best way to get color from each? For example, they might crush the berries and buds, and use a wet brush on the beets.

◉ Give each student a copy of page 53. Discuss the symbols the Plains Indians used to tell stories. Invite students to think of other symbols that might help tell a story.

◉ Using the reproducible as a guide, let students paint symbols on the brown paper to tell stories. Invite them to retell their stories using words.

Name That Color (Art, Language Arts)

Little Gopher tries to find just the right shades of color to paint the sunset. Let students help Little Gopher by experimenting with color mixing.

◎ Provide students with blue, yellow, red, white, and black tempera paint, paintbrushes, and bowls of water. Ask students to mix small amounts of paint on a sheet of white paper, experimenting with the way different amounts of black and white change the other colors.

◎ Once students have several color combinations they like, have them name them. For instance, a crisp green might be named *snap pea*. A fiery red-orange might be named *sunset* for the colors of a blazing sun setting in the sky. Have students cut out each color sample, paste it on a strip of paper, and record the descriptive color name.

◎ Create a color-word word wall by having students arrange their color swatches on posterboard. Display where students can see it while they are writing. Encourage them to use these descriptive color words when they describe color in their writing.

Pleasant Dream Catcher (Art)

Ask students if they've ever woken up and wished they could recall a pleasant dream. Native Americans had dream catchers just for that purpose. Hung above the head of a sleeping person, the weblike design "caught" the pleasant dreams on its threads, then gathered them like dew and dripped them down a feather into the mind of the person sleeping. Bad dreams and nightmares slipped through the holes.

Ask students to bring in plastic coffee can lids from home. Have them fold each lid in half and cut out the center of the lid. Then have students use a wide-gauge needle and lanyard or yarn to crisscross the cutout area, creating a web of brightly colored threads. Supply students with beads, feathers, and strips of leather to weave into their designs.

Dreamy Poetry (Language Arts)

Read aloud the poem "Sweet Dreams" without displaying it for students. Then take a few minutes to review the long-*e* sound (*e, ee, ea, y*), which is repeated in all but one line. Tell students that you will read the poem again, but this time they need to give you the thumbs-up symbol whenever they hear the long-*e* sound. Use this oral reading as an opportunity to observe students' developing phonemic awareness skills. To explore the poem's content, invite children to describe some of their happy dreams. Are ice cream and cake part of anyone's dreams?

Sweet Dreams

One night Neal went to sleep
And had a very happy dream.
He dreamed he ate three bowls
Of chocolate-chip ice cream.

The very next morning,
When Neal was wide awake,
He said, "Next time I dream,
I'd like to eat some cake!"

—*Linda B. Ross*

Name _____ Date _____

◆❋◆ Legend Organizer ◆❋◆

Use this sheet to record information about your legend.

Title: _____

Author: _____

List the characters and props, or objects, involved in the story.

(Characters)   (Props)

_____   _____

_____   _____

_____   _____

_____   _____

List the most important events from the story.

① _____

② _____

③ _____

Summary

Write a brief summary of the legend, telling what happens and why.

_____

_____

_____

_____

_____

Teaching With Favorite Tomie dePaola Books   Scholastic Teaching Resources

Painting a Story

Little Gopher used natural pigments to paint symbols on buckskin. These symbols told a story. Here are some symbols you can use to create your own story.

Retell your story with words.

_____

_____

_____

_____

_____

The
Art Lesson

Tomie dePaola

The Art Lesson

•

(P U T N A M   &   G R O S S E T ,   1 9 8 9)

After learning to be creative and drawing pictures at home, young Tommy is dismayed when he goes to school and finds the art lesson there much more regimented.

Concepts and Themes

▲▲▲▲▲▲

○ Individuality

○ Creativity

Before Reading

What do students know about "lessons"? What do they think an "art lesson" might be like? Encourage children to think about their own art lessons at school to predict what happens during the art lesson in this story. Judging from the expression on the boy's face in the cover illustration, how do students think this art lesson went?

During Reading

The expressions on the characters' faces in this story say a lot about what's happening. Take time to let children notice and discuss the facial expressions. Let them try making similar expressions. What feelings go with those faces? To build vocabulary for feelings, try naming a feeling, such as *proud*. As you read, challenge children to find an expression in an illustration that matches that word.

After Reading

Help students explore cause and effect with the following questions:

◎ Why is Tommy disappointed in kindergarten? (*for example, because he won't get art lessons until the next year; the paper at school gets wrinkly and the paint cracks*)

◎ What words describe how Tommy felt when the art teacher told the class everyone had to use the same crayons?

◎ What did Tommy think about copying the teacher's pilgrim? How do you know?

◎ Why do you think the art teacher finally decided to let Tommy draw his own picture with his own crayons?

◎ If you were the teacher, would you have let Tommy use his box of crayons? Why?

Imagination Murals (Art)

Invite students to draw on the walls just as Tommy did in the story. Display a large sheet of mural paper on a wall. Provide students with crayons, markers, pencils, or even some blue chalk like the chalk Tommy used in the story. Encourage children to let their imagination lead the way as they draw pictures. When the mural is complete, use it to inspire children's creative writing. Explain that this story is based on what happened to Tomie dePaola in kindergarten, that real events motivated his writing the book. When a student says, "What should I write about?" have the child go to the Imagination Mural, locate his or her own artwork, and write about the experience. To guide young writers you might post a question beneath the mural, asking students to describe their pictures or explain how it felt to draw whatever they wanted.

Story Scavenger Hunt (Language Arts)

Encourage connections to other books by Tomie dePaola by taking a close look at the last page of *The Art Lesson*. Can students name the books these illustrations are from? Plan a scavenger hunt to learn more. Take a trip to the school library and have children locate books by Tomie dePaola. How many illustrations can they match up to the pictures on the last page of *The Art Lesson*? Many of them appear in more than one book, including *Meet the Barkers: Morgan and Moffat Go to School*, *The Wind and the Sun*, *Strega Nona*, *Bill and Pete*, and *The Popcorn Book*. Borrow books students are not familiar with and add them to the class collection.

Crayon Acrostics (Language Arts)

Crayons are an important part of Tomie's life. In fact, in addition to thanking his fifth-grade teacher and his art teacher in the dedication, he thanks Binney & Smith Inc., makers of Crayola crayons. Celebrate crayons in the classroom with acrostic poems. Have students write "crayon" in capital letters vertically on a sheet of paper. For each letter, have students write a word that relates to crayons or drawing.

C ornflower blue
R ed
A mber
Y ellow
O range
N utmeg
S ea green

C olorful
R adiant
A wesome
Y ou can do it!
O riginal
N eat
S ensational

Tip

Make connections by discussing other books by Tomie dePaola in which students have met Grandma or other characters. (Students may remember her from *Watch Out for the Chicken Feet in Your Soup*, page 13.)

Book Links

The Art Box
by Gail Gibbons
(Holiday House, 1998)

Take a close-up look at the supplies found in an artist's box.

Draw Me a Star
by Eric Carle
(Paper Star, 1998)

A grandmother illustrates a star for a young boy and sets her grandson off on a lifetime of drawing.

Harold and the Purple Crayon
by Crockett Johnson
(Harper & Row, 1955)

Harold's imagination and one purple crayon take him into a world of adventure.

Someday Stories (Language Arts, Social Studies)

"Tommy knew he wanted to be an artist when he grew up." Reread these first words from the story to students. Ask: "What are some ways Tommy showed how much he wanted to be an artist?" Discuss the many ways Tommy pursued his dream—drawing pictures wherever he went, taking advice from his cousins in art school, displaying his art in lots of places, and trying out different colors. Invite children to tell about things they might like to do or be when they grow up. Discuss some of the ways people practice or learn to do those things. Let children write "Someday Stories" about their hopes and dreams and then illustrate them. They can use the beginning of *The Art Lesson* as inspiration, substituting their name for "Tommy" and changing "artist" to whatever word represents their dream. To illustrate their stories, children will surely enjoy an opportunity to explore one of Tomie dePaola's favorite artistic mediums...watercolor.

Painting a Picture (Art, Language Arts)

Share with students a playful poem about painting. Then let students try writing similar poems about their own painting.

◎ Give each child a copy of page 57. Read the poem aloud. Let students identify the rhyming words (*worm* and *squirm*) and other fun things about the poem.

◎ Provide watercolors and paintbrushes and let children complete the picture on the page, painting the apple and then making their paintbrush "wiggle" as the poet says, to make the worm "squirm."

◎ Invite children to paint their own simple pictures on another sheet of paper. They can use the poem as a model for telling the steps they followed and special techniques they used.

Painting a Picture

I paint an apple on the tree
And then I paint a worm.
I make my paintbrush wiggle
So the little worm will squirm.

—*Sandra Liatsos*

Tom

❖❖

(P U T N A M , 1 9 9 3)

This is a story about Tomie, as a youngster, and the trick his Irish grandfather taught him.

Concepts and Themes

▲▲▲▲▲▲▲

○ Family

○ Humor

○ Names

Before Reading

Invite children to make a prediction about the story. Ask: "Who do you think is pictured on the cover?" Draw attention to the character's clothing. Ask: "Do we wear clothes like this today?" Find out what students know about a shop like the one pictured on the cover. Ask: "What kind of store is the man in? Have you ever seen meat and chicken hanging in a shop?"

During Reading

Encourage attention to detail by exploring the illustrations in the book. Expand on students' observations about the shop on the cover by asking them to look for additional details in the book—for example, they might notice the roll of string, an old-fashioned scale, a butcher block, and a cash register. These sorts of observations will help students develop a sense of the story's setting.

After Reading

Revisit children's predictions, learn about genre, make connections to other stories, explore setting (time and place), and encourage reflection with these questions:

◎ Why do you think Tomie dePaola wrote this story?

◎ Have you read other stories by Tomie dePaola about a memory like this one? (Some examples are *The Art Lesson, Nana Upstairs & Nana Downstairs, Baby Sister, Watch Out for the Chicken Feet in Your Soup.*)

◎ Do the clothes Tom is wearing make sense now? Why?

◎ What words help describe this story? (For example, were parts of it funny, disgusting, familiar, or surprising?)

Eeek! Screech! (Language Arts)

"EEEK! EEEK! EEEK!" "Screech!" "Garunge-arunge-a!" "Whop Whop Whop." Use words from the story to build a word wall that teaches onomatopoeia (words that imitate the sounds they name) and reinforces phonemic awareness.

◎ Revisit the story, looking for words that represent sounds. Let students say the words, using their voices to express the full meaning. As students say the words, ask: "What letters and sounds do you hear?" Record the sounds phonetically.

◎ Brainstorm other words for sounds. Again, record the sounds phonetically as students name the letters and sounds they hear.

◎ Copy words for sounds on tagboard strips (or sentence strips). Arrange the words on a wall space. Encourage students to use these playful words to enliven their writing.

A New Adventure (Language Arts)

After discussing the story, brainstorm ideas about other pranks Tom and Tommy might think up. Use them for a class writing lesson.

◎ Record students' ideas on chart paper. Work together as a class to compose a new adventure based on these ideas. Encourage each child to participate and add a sentence or two.

◎ Follow the writing process through the creation of this newest adventure. Revise and edit on chart paper, an overhead, or a computer.

◎ Let students publish their adventure as a large collaborative book. As students prepare to illustrate their pages, revisit *Tom* to notice how Tomie dePaola framed his art. Students might like to try the same technique with their own illustrations.

Bigmama's
by Donald Crews
(Mulberry, 1998)
A man looks back with fondness and nostalgia at summers spent at his grandmother's home in Florida.

My Ol' Man
by Patricia Polacco
(Philomel Books, 1995)
Two siblings become convinced a magic rock found by their father will help him get his job back.

Shortcut
by Donald Crews
(Mulberry, 1996)
One afternoon a group of childhood friends decide to take a shortcut along the railroad track and get more than they'd bargained for.

Tip

Make Individual Books

Students might like to copy the collaborative text into smaller books and illustrate the pages to make books they can share at home.

Story Sequence Cube (Language Arts)

Make story sequence cubes to explore the sequence of events in *Tom*.

◎ Give each student a copy of page 62. Have students use pictures to record what happened in the story in the correct order, beginning with box 1 and ending with box 6. Students may find it helpful to plan what they will show on a separate sheet of paper.

◎ Have students glue the reproducible to sturdy paper and cut along the solid lines. Guide students in folding along the dotted lines to form a cube. Have them secure the edges with glue or tape.

◎ Invite students to share their cubes with a partner, retelling the events of the story and practicing oral language skills. Have students discuss similarities and differences among their cubes. To encourage discussion, ask: "Why is it easier to remember some events in the story more clearly than others? What strategies did you use to figure out what happened first? Second?"

Snapshot Stories (Language Arts)

Tommy enjoyed it when Tom told him funny family stories as well as stories he made up. Ask: "Why do you think Tommy cherished those times? Does your family or someone close to you share favorite stories?" Photographs are wonderful springboards for a mini-lesson on personal narratives that draw on these stories.

◎ Begin by giving students an interactive homework assignment: Ask them to bring in a snapshot from home or to draw a picture of a favorite activity they've shared with their family or someone close to them.

◎ Use the pictures as inspiration for writing. Ask: "What's happening in that picture?" Let children dictate or write stories that go with their pictures. Encourage them to think about who is telling the story (point of view), what the reader can learn about the character(s), and what details will help the reader imagine being there.

◎ Have children create fun frames for their photos by folding a sheet of colorful paper and cutting out the center to fit the photo. Or cut construction paper into triangles to make photo corners. Have children glue only the outer edges of the corners to a sheet of paper and then slip the photos inside to secure.

Clothespin Graph (Math)

To help students evaluate what they've read, record the following question at the top of a 12- by 18-inch sheet of tagboard: "Was it a good idea for Tommy to bring chicken feet to school?" Set up a clothespin graph for students to record their answers:

◎ Divide the tagboard in half vertically.

◎ Write the word "Yes" at the top of one column and "No" at the top of the other column.

◎ Number the left and right sides of the graph 1–20 (or higher, depending on how many students you have).

◎ Invite children to clip their clothespins to the graph to answer the question and express their opinions. Discuss students' reasoning and what the graph shows.

Tip

▲▲▲▲▲▲▲

This story isn't the only place readers will find a mention of chicken feet. Invite children to make a connection after reading *Watch Out for the Chicken Feet in Your Soup.* (See page 13.)

Special People Poems (Language Arts)

In this poem, the author (a child) compares hugging Grandma and Grandpa to hugging the trees she loves to climb. Encourage students to think about how they feel about someone they love. Ask, "What do you think of when you see this person? When you give this person a hug, does it remind you of something?" Invite students to write down their ideas in a free-verse format and illustrate them.

Loving

When I see Grandma and Grandpa.
When I climb up trees.
I can hug trees.
They feel like wood.
Grandpa and Grandma don't feel like wood.
They feel like smooth skin.

—Nekeia

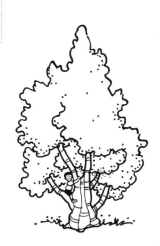

Story
Sequence
Cube

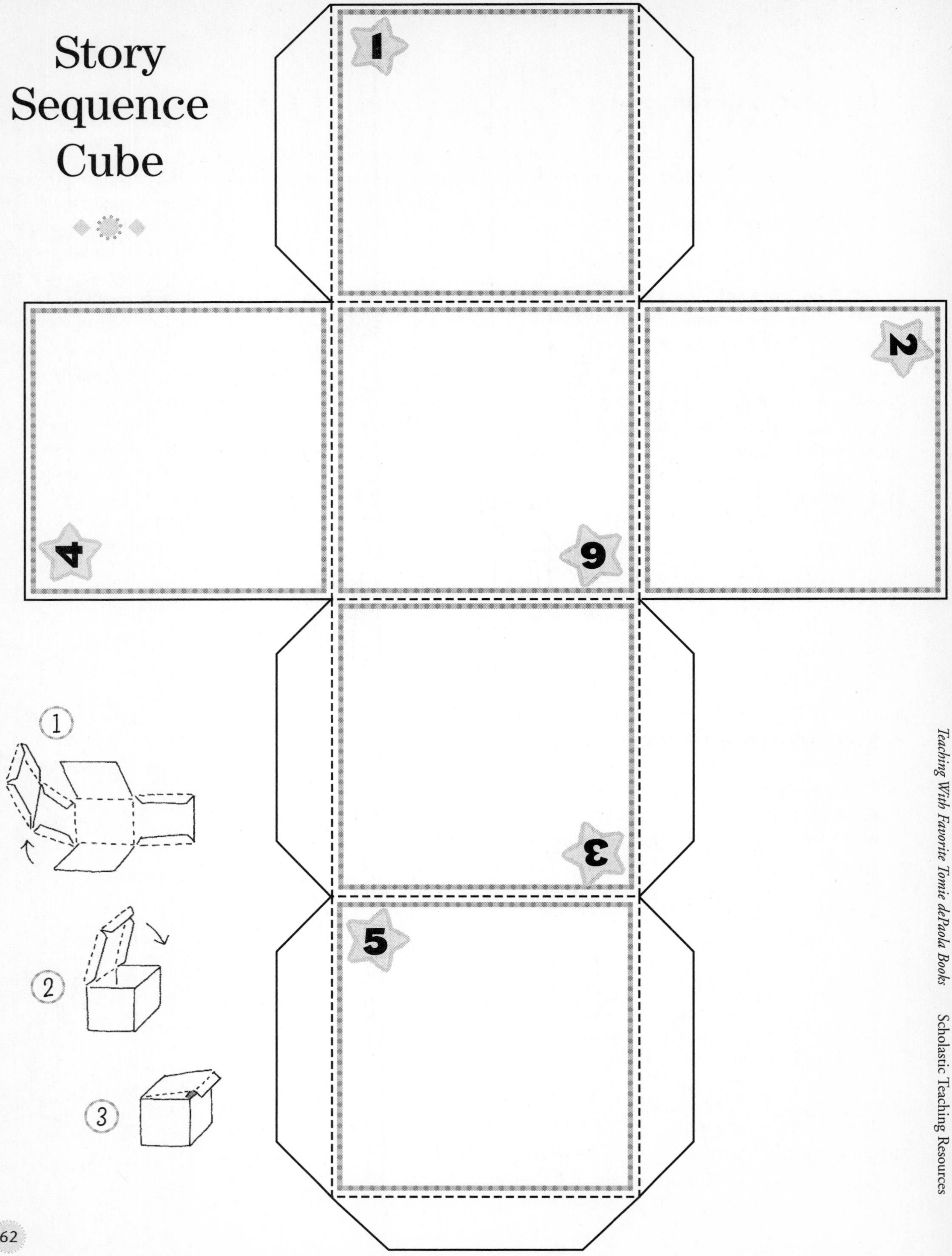

◆ ❋ ◆

1

2

4

6

3

5

①

②

③

Teaching With Favorite Tomie dePaola Books

Scholastic Teaching Resources

Learn More With Other Tomie dePaola Books

Nana Upstairs & Nana Downstairs

(PUTNAM, 1973)

Tommy enjoys his relationship with both his grandmother and great-grandmother. With his family's support he copes with his great-grandmother's death.

Extending the Book

A Feelings Chart: Draw the outline of a house on chart paper. Draw a line horizontally to divide the house into an upstairs and downstairs. On the top floor, record words that describe how Tommy felt about Nana Upstairs. On the bottom floor, record words that describe how Tommy felt about Nana Downstairs. Invite students to find evidence of Tommy's feelings in the text. Take a few minutes to talk about feelings and how we express them. Tomie dePaola shared how he felt about his grandmother and great-grandmother by writing this book. Ask: "What are some other ways people may express feelings?"

The Quicksand Book

(HOLIDAY HOUSE, 1977)

As a girl slowly sinks in quicksand, a boy shares with the reader his extensive knowledge of quicksand. This funny and informative page-turner is a great introduction to nonfiction.

Extending the Book

Experts Speak: The boy in this story delivers a lecture about quicksand, made suspenseful because of the girl who is at that very moment sinking. Let students have fun delivering a "lecture" about something they are experts on. This could be a hobby they have, a subject they're especially interested in, or a topic they're researching for class. Preparing for these mini-lectures reinforces organization skills, as children decide what information to include and in what order. They'll also have to think about what to leave out, so listeners won't lose interest. Children will practice speaking skills as they present their lectures, while members of the audience will hone listening skills. A lectern makes a fun prop. Children with visual aids may also enjoy using a pointer.

Bonjour, Mr. Satie

(PUTNAM, 1991)

There is an art competition between the feuding Pablo and Henri (Picasso and Matisse), and Mr. Satie is called on to referee. His tactful approach lets each artist emerge a winner.

Extending the Book

Name That Person! Research Project: The last pages of this book feature a crowd of famous faces, including James Joyce, Isadora Duncan, Calvin Coolidge, Pablo Picasso, Ernest Hemingway, and Claude Monet. Visit the library to hone research skills and learn about each person's claim to fame. This lesson spans art, writing, politics, history, and music.

Kit and Kat

(PRICE STERN PUBLISHERS, 1994)

This collection of short chapters follows the adventures of a feline brother and sister as they head to their grandparents' house for a sleepover, learn to ride bicycles, and deal with the class bully.

Extending the Book

Listen, Stop, Draw, Discuss! Use drawings to help check students' comprehension. Begin by distributing drawing paper to children. Have each student fold his or her paper in half, turn the page, and then fold it in half again. When unfolded, the paper should have four square-shaped sections. Ask children to number each one with the numerals 1 through 4. Explain that as you share the book aloud, you'll stop reading four times. Each time you'll ask students to draw a picture in one of the boxes. The picture should show the events from the story. (Rather than showing the book's illustrations to children, allow students to create their own mental pictures.) When children are ready, begin the activity. Read a few pages of the story and stop. Ask children to draw a picture to show what's happening. To check comprehension, you may want to ask for volunteers to describe their drawings. Or observe what individual children draw and invite them to explain the illustration. For example, after reading the first few pages of "Kat's Good Idea," one student might draw Kit with a sad facial expression sitting on a blue bike. After the drawings are complete, have children write a sentence below each picture, describing the scene.

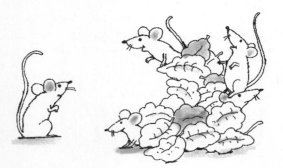

Baby Sister

(PUTNAM, 1996)

Tommy's mother is expecting a baby, so Italian Nana comes for a visit.

Extending the Book

Learn About Life Cycles: Have children fold a sheet of paper in half and draw a line on the fold to divide the paper into two sections. On one half, ask them to draw a picture of themselves as a baby and complete the sentence: When I was a baby I could _____ . On the other half, have them draw a picture of themselves as they are now and complete the sentence: Now I can _____ ! Discuss other ways children have changed.

Mice Squeak, We Speak

(PUTNAM, 1997)

In Tomie dePaola's illustrated version of a lively poem by Arnold L. Shapiro, animals squeak, neigh, cluck, hoot, hum, bleat, creak, squeal, and screech. They even speak! All of this noise will surely encourage children to chime in on a read-aloud of the story. Illustrations include details about each animal's habitat, inviting children to make comparisons and learn more.

Extending the Book

Syllable-Count Sorting: Increase awareness of word parts with this counting and sorting game. Begin by making a four-column chart. Across the horizontal axis, write "How Many Syllables Do We Hear?" Label the columns 1, 2, 3, and 4. Have children recall the names of the animals from the story, and clap the number of syllables. Write the name of the animal in the corresponding column. For example, bats would go in the "1" column, crickets in the "2" column, and coyote in the "3" column. To learn more with the animal names, sort by predominant vowels.